this

notebook

BELONGS TO:

．．．

DATE:

．．．

"Nature does not hurry, yet everything is accomplished."

LAO TZU

index

	PAGE

4

index

DATE: _____ TIME: _____

VENUE: _____

NO. OF
ATTENDEES: _____

PRIVATE CLASS: Y / N

THEME/FOCUS:

PROPS

NOTES

OILS

MUSIC

FEEDBACK

☆ ☆ ☆ ☆ ☆

MANTRA / POSITIVE QUOTE:

lesson
SEQUENCE

DATE: _____ TIME: _____

VENUE: _____

NO. OF
ATTENDEES: _____

PRIVATE CLASS: Y / N

THEME/FOCUS:

NOTES

PROPS

OILS

MUSIC

FEEDBACK

☆ ☆ ☆ ☆ ☆

MANTRA / POSITIVE QUOTE:

lesson
SEQUENCE

DATE: _____ TIME: _____

VENUE: _____

THEME/FOCUS:

PROPS

OILS

MUSIC

NOTES

FEEDBACK

☆ ☆ ☆ ☆ ☆

MANTRA / POSITIVE QUOTE:

lesson
SEQUENCE

DATE: _____ TIME: _____

VENUE: _____

THEME/FOCUS:

· PROPS ·

OILS

MUSIC

NOTES

FEEDBACK

☆ ☆ ☆ ☆ ☆

MANTRA / POSITIVE QUOTE:

lesson
SEQUENCE

DATE: _____ TIME: _____

VENUE: _____

NO. OF ATTENDEES: _____

PRIVATE CLASS: Y / N

THEME/FOCUS:

· PROPS ·

NOTES

FEEDBACK

OILS

MUSIC

☆ ☆ ☆ ☆ ☆

MANTRA / POSITIVE QUOTE:

lesson
SEQUENCE

DATE: _____ TIME: _____

VENUE: _____

NO. OF
ATTENDEES: _____

PRIVATE CLASS: Y / N

THEME/FOCUS:

PROPS

NOTES

OILS

MUSIC

FEEDBACK

☆ ☆ ☆ ☆ ☆

MANTRA / POSITIVE QUOTE:

lesson
SEQUENCE

DATE: _____ TIME: _____

VENUE: _____

NO. OF
ATTENDEES: _____

PRIVATE CLASS: Y / N

THEME/FOCUS:

PROPS

OILS

MUSIC

NOTES

FEEDBACK

☆ ☆ ☆ ☆ ☆

MANTRA / POSITIVE QUOTE:

lesson SEQUENCE

DATE: _____ TIME: _____

VENUE: _____

THEME/FOCUS:

PROPS

NOTES

OILS

MUSIC

FEEDBACK

☆ ☆ ☆ ☆ ☆

MANTRA / POSITIVE QUOTE:

lesson SEQUENCE

DATE: _____ TIME: _____

VENUE: _____

NO. OF
ATTENDEES: _____

PRIVATE CLASS: Y / N

THEME/FOCUS:

· PROPS ·

NOTES

OILS

MUSIC

FEEDBACK

☆ ☆ ☆ ☆ ☆

MANTRA / POSITIVE QUOTE:

lesson
SEQUENCE

DATE: _____ TIME: _____

VENUE: _____

NO. OF
ATTENDEES: _____

PRIVATE CLASS: Y / N

THEME/FOCUS:

PROPS

NOTES

OILS

MUSIC

FEEDBACK

☆ ☆ ☆ ☆ ☆

MANTRA / POSITIVE QUOTE:

lesson
SEQUENCE

DATE: _____ TIME: _____

VENUE: _____

THEME/FOCUS:

NO. OF
ATTENDEES: _____

PRIVATE CLASS: Y / N

NOTES

· PROPS ·

OILS

MUSIC

FEEDBACK

☆ ☆ ☆ ☆ ☆

MANTRA / POSITIVE QUOTE:

SEQUENCE

DATE: _____ TIME: _____

VENUE: _____

THEME/FOCUS:

PROPS

NOTES

OILS

MUSIC

FEEDBACK

☆ ☆ ☆ ☆ ☆

MANTRA / POSITIVE QUOTE:

lesson
SEQUENCE

DATE: _____ TIME: _____

VENUE: _____

NO. OF
ATTENDEES: _____

PRIVATE CLASS: Y / N

THEME/FOCUS:

PROPS

OILS

MUSIC

NOTES

FEEDBACK

☆ ☆ ☆ ☆ ☆

MANTRA / POSITIVE QUOTE:

lesson
SEQUENCE

DATE: _____ TIME: _____

VENUE: _____

NO. OF
ATTENDEES: _____

PRIVATE CLASS: Y / N

THEME/FOCUS:

NOTES

· PROPS ·

FEEDBACK

OILS

MUSIC

☆ ☆ ☆ ☆ ☆

MANTRA / POSITIVE QUOTE:

SEQUENCE

DATE: _____ TIME: _____

VENUE: _____

NO. OF
ATTENDEES: _____

PRIVATE CLASS: Y / N

THEME/FOCUS:

PROPS

NOTES

OILS

MUSIC

FEEDBACK

☆ ☆ ☆ ☆ ☆

MANTRA / POSITIVE QUOTE:

lesson
SEQUENCE

DATE: _____ TIME: _____

VENUE: _____

THEME/FOCUS:

NO. OF
ATTENDEES: _____

PRIVATE CLASS: Y / N

NOTES

· PROPS ·

OILS

MUSIC

FEEDBACK

☆ ☆ ☆ ☆ ☆

MANTRA / POSITIVE QUOTE:

lesson
SEQUENCE

DATE: _____ TIME: _____

VENUE: _____

NO. OF
ATTENDEES: _____

PRIVATE CLASS: Y / N

THEME/FOCUS:

· PROPS ·

NOTES

OILS

MUSIC

FEEDBACK

☆ ☆ ☆ ☆ ☆

MANTRA / POSITIVE QUOTE:

lesson
SEQUENCE

DATE: _____ TIME: _____

VENUE: _____

NO. OF ATTENDEES: _____

PRIVATE CLASS: Y / N

THEME/FOCUS:

PROPS

NOTES

OILS

MUSIC

FEEDBACK

☆ ☆ ☆ ☆ ☆

MANTRA / POSITIVE QUOTE:

SEQUENCE

DATE: _____ TIME: _____

VENUE: _____

NO. OF ATTENDEES: _____

PRIVATE CLASS: Y / N

THEME/FOCUS:

PROPS

NOTES

OILS

MUSIC

FEEDBACK

☆ ☆ ☆ ☆ ☆

MANTRA / POSITIVE QUOTE:

SEQUENCE

DATE: _____ TIME: _____

VENUE: _____

THEME/FOCUS:

NO. OF
ATTENDEES: _____

PRIVATE CLASS: Y / N

NOTES

PROPS

OILS

MUSIC

FEEDBACK

☆ ☆ ☆ ☆ ☆

MANTRA / POSITIVE QUOTE:

lesson SEQUENCE

DATE: _____ TIME: _____

VENUE: _____

NO. OF
ATTENDEES: _____

PRIVATE CLASS: Y / N

THEME/FOCUS:

PROPS

NOTES

OILS

MUSIC

FEEDBACK

☆ ☆ ☆ ☆ ☆

MANTRA / POSITIVE QUOTE:

46

lesson
SEQUENCE

DATE: _____ TIME: _____

VENUE: _____

NO. OF
ATTENDEES: _____

PRIVATE CLASS: Y / N

THEME/FOCUS:

· PROPS ·

OILS

MUSIC

NOTES

FEEDBACK

☆ ☆ ☆ ☆ ☆

MANTRA / POSITIVE QUOTE:

lesson
SEQUENCE

DATE: _____ TIME: _____

VENUE: _____

NO. OF ATTENDEES: _____

PRIVATE CLASS: Y / N

THEME/FOCUS:

· PROPS ·

NOTES

FEEDBACK

OILS

MUSIC

☆ ☆ ☆ ☆ ☆

MANTRA / POSITIVE QUOTE:

lesson
SEQUENCE

DATE: _____ TIME: _____

VENUE: _____

NO. OF
ATTENDEES: _____

PRIVATE CLASS: Y / N

THEME/FOCUS:

PROPS

NOTES

OILS

MUSIC

FEEDBACK

☆ ☆ ☆ ☆ ☆

MANTRA / POSITIVE QUOTE:

lesson
SEQUENCE

DATE: _____ TIME: _____

VENUE: _____

NO. OF
ATTENDEES: _____

PRIVATE CLASS: Y / N

THEME/FOCUS:

PROPS

NOTES

OILS

MUSIC

FEEDBACK

☆ ☆ ☆ ☆ ☆

MANTRA / POSITIVE QUOTE:

lesson
SEQUENCE

DATE: _____ TIME: _____

VENUE: _____

THEME/FOCUS:

· PROPS ·

OILS

MUSIC

NO. OF
ATTENDEES: _____

PRIVATE CLASS: Y / N

NOTES

FEEDBACK

☆ ☆ ☆ ☆ ☆

MANTRA / POSITIVE QUOTE:

SEQUENCE

DATE: _____ TIME: _____

VENUE: _____

NO. OF
ATTENDEES: _____

PRIVATE CLASS: Y / N

THEME/FOCUS:

PROPS

NOTES

OILS

MUSIC

FEEDBACK

☆ ☆ ☆ ☆ ☆

MANTRA / POSITIVE QUOTE:

lesson
SEQUENCE

DATE: _____ TIME: _____

VENUE: _____

NO. OF
ATTENDEES: _____

PRIVATE CLASS: Y / N

THEME/FOCUS:

· PROPS ·

OILS

MUSIC

NOTES

FEEDBACK

☆ ☆ ☆ ☆ ☆

MANTRA / POSITIVE QUOTE:

lesson
SEQUENCE

DATE: _____ TIME: _____

VENUE: _____

NO. OF
ATTENDEES: _____

PRIVATE CLASS: Y / N

THEME/FOCUS:

PROPS

NOTES

OILS

MUSIC

FEEDBACK

☆ ☆ ☆ ☆ ☆

MANTRA / POSITIVE QUOTE:

lesson
SEQUENCE

DATE: _____ TIME: _____

VENUE: _____

NO. OF
ATTENDEES: _____

PRIVATE CLASS: Y / N

THEME/FOCUS:

PROPS · · · · · · · · · · ·

OILS

MUSIC

NOTES

FEEDBACK

☆ ☆ ☆ ☆ ☆

MANTRA / POSITIVE QUOTE:

SEQUENCE

DATE: _____ TIME: _____

VENUE: _____

NO. OF ATTENDEES: _____

PRIVATE CLASS: Y / N

THEME/FOCUS:

PROPS

NOTES

OILS

MUSIC

FEEDBACK

☆ ☆ ☆ ☆ ☆

MANTRA / POSITIVE QUOTE:

lesson
SEQUENCE

DATE: _____ TIME: _____

VENUE: _____

NO. OF
ATTENDEES: _____

PRIVATE CLASS: Y / N

THEME/FOCUS:

· PROPS · · · · · · · · · · · · ·

NOTES

OILS

MUSIC

FEEDBACK

☆ ☆ ☆ ☆ ☆

MANTRA / POSITIVE QUOTE:

lesson
SEQUENCE

DATE: _____ TIME: _____

VENUE: _____

NO. OF
ATTENDEES: _____

PRIVATE CLASS: Y / N

THEME/FOCUS:

PROPS

NOTES

OILS

MUSIC

FEEDBACK

☆ ☆ ☆ ☆ ☆

MANTRA / POSITIVE QUOTE:

lesson
SEQUENCE

DATE: _____ TIME: _____

VENUE: _____

NO. OF
ATTENDEES: _____

PRIVATE CLASS: Y / N

THEME/FOCUS:

PROPS

OILS

MUSIC

NOTES

FEEDBACK

☆ ☆ ☆ ☆ ☆

MANTRA / POSITIVE QUOTE:

lesson
SEQUENCE

DATE: _____ TIME: _____

VENUE: _____

NO. OF ATTENDEES: _____

PRIVATE CLASS: Y / N

THEME/FOCUS:

PROPS

OILS

MUSIC

NOTES

FEEDBACK

☆ ☆ ☆ ☆ ☆

MANTRA / POSITIVE QUOTE:

lesson
SEQUENCE

DATE: _____ TIME: _____

VENUE: _____

NO. OF
ATTENDEES: _____

PRIVATE CLASS: Y / N

THEME/FOCUS:

PROPS

NOTES

OILS

MUSIC

FEEDBACK

☆ ☆ ☆ ☆ ☆

MANTRA / POSITIVE QUOTE:

SEQUENCE

DATE: _____ TIME: _____

VENUE: _____

NO. OF
ATTENDEES: _____

PRIVATE CLASS: Y / N

THEME/FOCUS:

PROPS

NOTES

OILS

MUSIC

FEEDBACK

☆ ☆ ☆ ☆ ☆

MANTRA / POSITIVE QUOTE:

lesson
SEQUENCE

DATE: _____ TIME: _____

VENUE: _____

NO. OF ATTENDEES: _____

PRIVATE CLASS: Y / N

THEME/FOCUS:

· PROPS ·

OILS

MUSIC

NOTES

FEEDBACK

☆ ☆ ☆ ☆ ☆

MANTRA / POSITIVE QUOTE:

lesson
SEQUENCE

DATE: _____ TIME: _____

VENUE: _____

NO. OF ATTENDEES: _____

PRIVATE CLASS: Y / N

THEME/FOCUS:

PROPS

NOTES

OILS

MUSIC

FEEDBACK

☆ ☆ ☆ ☆ ☆

MANTRA / POSITIVE QUOTE:

SEQUENCE

DATE: _____ TIME: _____

VENUE: _____

NO. OF ATTENDEES: _____

PRIVATE CLASS: Y / N

THEME/FOCUS:

PROPS

OILS

MUSIC

NOTES

FEEDBACK

☆ ☆ ☆ ☆ ☆

MANTRA / POSITIVE QUOTE:

SEQUENCE

DATE: _____ TIME: _____

VENUE: _____

NO. OF
ATTENDEES: _____

PRIVATE CLASS: Y / N

THEME/FOCUS:

· PROPS ·

OILS

MUSIC

NOTES

FEEDBACK

☆ ☆ ☆ ☆ ☆

MANTRA / POSITIVE QUOTE:

lesson
SEQUENCE

DATE: _____ TIME: _____

VENUE: _____

NO. OF
ATTENDEES: _____

PRIVATE CLASS: Y / N

THEME/FOCUS:

PROPS

NOTES

OILS

MUSIC

FEEDBACK

☆ ☆ ☆ ☆ ☆

MANTRA / POSITIVE QUOTE:

lesson
SEQUENCE

DATE: _____ TIME: _____

VENUE: _____

NO. OF ATTENDEES: _____

PRIVATE CLASS: Y / N

THEME/FOCUS:

· PROPS ·

OILS

MUSIC

NOTES

FEEDBACK

☆ ☆ ☆ ☆ ☆

MANTRA / POSITIVE QUOTE:

lesson
SEQUENCE

DATE: _____ TIME: _____

VENUE: _____

NO. OF
ATTENDEES: _____

PRIVATE CLASS: Y / N

THEME/FOCUS:

NOTES

PROPS

OILS

MUSIC

FEEDBACK

☆ ☆ ☆ ☆ ☆

MANTRA / POSITIVE QUOTE:

lesson
SEQUENCE

DATE: _____ TIME: _____

VENUE: _____

NO. OF
ATTENDEES: _____

PRIVATE CLASS: Y / N

THEME/FOCUS:

PROPS

OILS

MUSIC

NOTES

FEEDBACK

☆ ☆ ☆ ☆ ☆

MANTRA / POSITIVE QUOTE:

SEQUENCE

DATE: _____ TIME: _____

VENUE: _____

THEME/FOCUS:

NOTES

PROPS

OILS

MUSIC

FEEDBACK

☆ ☆ ☆ ☆ ☆

MANTRA / POSITIVE QUOTE:

lesson
SEQUENCE

DATE: _____ TIME: _____

VENUE: _____

NO. OF
ATTENDEES: _____

PRIVATE CLASS: Y / N

THEME/FOCUS:

PROPS

OILS

MUSIC

NOTES

FEEDBACK

☆ ☆ ☆ ☆ ☆

MANTRA / POSITIVE QUOTE:

lesson
SEQUENCE

DATE: _____ TIME: _____

VENUE: _____

NO. OF ATTENDEES: _____

PRIVATE CLASS: Y / N

THEME/FOCUS:

PROPS

NOTES

OILS

MUSIC

FEEDBACK

☆ ☆ ☆ ☆ ☆

MANTRA / POSITIVE QUOTE:

lesson
SEQUENCE

DATE: _____ TIME: _____

VENUE: _____

NO. OF
ATTENDEES: _____

PRIVATE CLASS: Y / N

THEME/FOCUS:

NOTES

· PROPS ·

OILS

MUSIC

FEEDBACK

☆ ☆ ☆ ☆ ☆

MANTRA / POSITIVE QUOTE:

SEQUENCE

DATE: _____ TIME: _____

VENUE: _____

NO. OF
ATTENDEES: _____

PRIVATE CLASS: Y / N

THEME/FOCUS:

NOTES

PROPS

OILS

MUSIC

FEEDBACK

☆ ☆ ☆ ☆ ☆

MANTRA / POSITIVE QUOTE:

lesson
SEQUENCE

DATE: _____ TIME: _____

VENUE: _____

NO. OF
ATTENDEES: _____

PRIVATE CLASS: Y / N

THEME/FOCUS:

PROPS

OILS

MUSIC

NOTES

FEEDBACK

☆ ☆ ☆ ☆ ☆

MANTRA / POSITIVE QUOTE:

lesson
SEQUENCE

DATE: _____ TIME: _____

VENUE: _____

NO. OF
ATTENDEES: _____

PRIVATE CLASS: Y / N

THEME/FOCUS:

PROPS ·

NOTES

FEEDBACK

OILS

MUSIC

☆ ☆ ☆ ☆ ☆

MANTRA / POSITIVE QUOTE:

lesson
SEQUENCE

119

Made in the USA
Monee, IL
28 February 2022